THE STATES AND THEIR SYMBOLS

South Dakota
Facts and Symbols

by Kathy Feeney

Consultant:
Mary B. Edelen
Director
South Dakota State Historical Society

Hilltop Books
an imprint of Capstone Press
Mankato, Minnesota

Hilltop Books are published by Capstone Press
151 Good Counsel Drive, P.O. Box 669, Mankato, Minnesota 56002
http://www.capstone-press.com

Library of Congress Cataloging-in-Publication Data
Feeney, Kathy, 1954–
  South Dakota facts and symbols/by Kathy Feeney.
  p. cm.—(The states and their symbols)
  Includes bibliographical references and index.
  Summary: Presents information about the state of South Dakota, its nickname,
motto, and emblems.
  ISBN 0-7368-0646-6
  1. Emblems, State—South Dakota—Juvenile literature. [1. Emblems, State—South
Dakota. 2. South Dakota.] I. Title. II. Series.
CR203.S8 F44 2001
978.3—dc21   00-022426

Editorial Credits

Karen L. Daas, editor; Linda Clavel, production designer and illustrator;
  Kimberly Danger and Heidi Schoof, photo researchers

Photo Credits

Jack Olson, 22 (bottom)
Kent and Donna Dannen, 18, 22 (middle)
One Mile Up, Inc., 8, 10 (inset)
Root Resources/Jim Flynn, 12
South Dakota Tourism, 14, 22 (top)
Tom Till Photography, 6
Unicorn Stock Photos/MacDonald Photography, 10
Visuals Unlimited/Tom Edwards, cover; John Bishop, 16; Ken Lucas, 20

1 2 3 4 5 6 06 05 04 03 02 01

Table of Contents

Fast Facts

Capital: Pierre is the capital of South Dakota.

Largest City: Sioux Falls is the largest city in South Dakota. About 110,270 people live there.

Size: South Dakota covers 77,121 square miles (199,743 square kilometers). It is the 17th largest state.

Location: South Dakota is in the midwestern United States. The state is in the northern Great Plains region.

Population: 733,133 people live in South Dakota (U.S. Census Bureau, 1999 estimate).

Statehood: On November 2, 1889, South Dakota became the 40th state to join the United States.

Natural Resources: South Dakota's most valuable natural resource is gold. The state has one of the largest gold mines in the world.

Manufactured Goods: South Dakota businesses produce electrical equipment, computers, and machinery.

Crops: Farmers in South Dakota grow corn, soybeans, sunflowers, and wheat. They also raise cattle, chickens, hogs, sheep, and buffalo.

State Name and Nickname

South Dakota's name comes from the Sioux Nation. The Teton, Yankton, and Santee tribes make up the Sioux Nation. This group of Native Americans calls themselves the Dakota. Dakota means friend. Members of the Sioux Nation still live in South Dakota today.

South Dakota's nickname is the Mount Rushmore State. Mount Rushmore National Memorial is in South Dakota's Black Hills.

Some people call South Dakota the Sunshine State. The Sunshine State was South Dakota's official state nickname from 1909 to 1992.

Another nickname for South Dakota is the Coyote State. The coyote is South Dakota's state animal. Coyotes live throughout the state.

People also call South Dakota the Land of Infinite Variety. The state has grassy plains, hills, mountains, and rocks.

The faces of U.S. Presidents George Washington, Thomas Jefferson, Theodore Roosevelt, and Abraham Lincoln are carved into Mount Rushmore National Memorial.

State Seal and Motto

South Dakota's government adopted its state seal in 1885. They chose a color version of the state seal in 1961. The seal represents South Dakota's government. The seal also makes government papers official.

South Dakota's state seal shows two pieces of land divided by a river. The Missouri River runs through South Dakota. A steamboat on the river represents trade and transportation.

The seal shows the importance of farming and manufacturing in South Dakota. A farming scene is on the right side of the river. Farming is an important business for South Dakotans. Manufacturing also is an important business in the state. A mill and furnace to the left of the river stand for manufacturing.

A banner appears above the river. South Dakota's state motto appears on the banner. The state's motto is "Under God the People Rule."

The year 1889 appears on South Dakota's state seal. South Dakota became a state in 1889. State officials added the date to the seal at that time.

State Capitol and Flag

Pierre is the capital of South Dakota. South Dakota's capitol building is in Pierre. Government officials meet there to make the state's laws.

Workers began to build South Dakota's capitol in 1904. They used limestone to construct the building. Workers completed the capitol in 1910. They later added a section to the building in 1932.

South Dakota's capitol has two domes. The inner dome is 96 feet (29 meters) tall. This dome is made of stained glass. The outer dome is copper. It is 159 feet (48 meters) tall.

South Dakota has had three state flags. Officials adopted the current state flag in 1992. The flag has a blue background. South Dakota's state seal is in the center of the flag. The state's name and motto form a circle around the state seal. "South Dakota, The Mount Rushmore State" appears in gold letters on the flag.

Minneapolis architects C.E. Bell and M.S. Detwiler designed South Dakota's state capitol. Their design was based on Montana's capitol.

11

State Bird

The ring-necked pheasant became South Dakota's state bird in 1943. The ring-necked pheasant is native to China. Explorers brought the bird to South Dakota in the 1880s. By 1944, ring-necked pheasants were so common in South Dakota that people called the state the Pheasant Capital of the World.

Many South Dakotans hunt wild male ring-necked pheasants. State laws protect females. People cannot hunt female ring-necked pheasants.

Male ring-necked pheasants grow to be about 33 inches (84 centimeters) long. They are black, brown, and white. They have a glossy blue-green neck. Blue-green feathers cover their head. Males have a white ring around their neck.

Female ring-necked pheasants have brown spotted bodies. They grow to be about 21 inches (53 centimeters) long. Females build their nests in tall grass. They lay as many as 13 eggs at one time.

Some South Dakota farmers raise ring-necked pheasants.

State Tree

South Dakota officials selected the Black Hills spruce as the state tree in 1947. This tree grows throughout South Dakota's Black Hills.

The Black Hills spruce is a member of the white spruce family of trees. White spruce wood is light yellow beneath the bark. Unlike other types of white spruce, the Black Hills spruce grows only in South Dakota.

Needles and cones grow on Black Hills spruce trees. The tree's needles are short and thick. Their color ranges from blue-green to bright green. Heavy wood cones grow on the Black Hills spruce. The cones hold seeds.

South Dakotans make paper, houses, and telephone poles from Black Hills spruce. People also plant Black Hills spruce in their yards. Farmers plant Black Hills spruce to help protect crops from the wind.

Black Hills spruce can grow to be 75 feet (23 meters) tall.

State Flower

Government officials named the American pasque flower South Dakota's state flower in 1903. This wildflower grows in many areas of South Dakota.

Pasque flowers grow well in the dry soil of South Dakota's prairies. The flowers have small purple blossoms. Long white silky hairs cover the flower.

Pasque is the French word for Easter. The pasque flower blooms about the same time as this spring holiday. People color Easter eggs with pasque flower dye.

People sometimes call American pasque flowers windflowers. Wind spreads the pasque flower's seeds across the prairie.

South Dakota's state flower is part of the state floral emblem. The words "I Lead" and a picture of the pasque flower make up the emblem.

People sometimes call American pasque flowers May Day flowers. The flowers usually bloom in April or May.

The coyote became South Dakota's official animal in 1949. Coyotes live throughout the state. They are most common along the Missouri River and in the Black Hills.

Coyotes are members of the dog family. Coyotes have gray fur. Their bushy gray tails are black at the tip. Coyotes' snouts are long and slender. Coyotes have slanted yellow eyes and broad, pointed ears.

Coyotes are carnivores. They eat meat with their sharp teeth. Coyotes hunt birds, chipmunks, and mice. They also catch rabbits, squirrels, and woodchucks. Coyotes often hunt for food in groups called packs. Coyotes have poor eyesight. They rely on their senses of smell and hearing to find food.

Female coyotes usually give birth to five to seven cubs at a time. Male and female coyotes share the responsibility of raising their young. They protect their young from danger.

Coyotes howl to contact their young and other coyotes.

More State Symbols

State Fish: The walleye became South Dakota's official state fish in 1982. This game fish is found in northeastern lakes and in the Missouri River.

State Fossil: South Dakota fifth grade students first suggested Triceratops as the state fossil. State officials adopted the symbol in 1988. The skeleton of a Triceratops was discovered in South Dakota in 1927. It is on display at Rapid City's Museum of Geology.

State Gemstone: The Fairburn agate became South Dakota's state gemstone in 1966. The gemstone is named for the town of Fairburn. The Fairburn agate is colorful. It has white swirls with bands of black, blue-gray, brown, pink, red, or yellow.

State Grass: Officials adopted western wheatgrass as South Dakota's state grass in 1970. People plant western wheatgrass to cover bare areas of land and to repair wildlife habitats.

Many South Dakotans fish for walleyes.

Places to Visit

Badlands National Park

Badlands National Park is in southwestern South Dakota. This region has steep canyons, colorful rocks, sharp spires, and grassy prairies. Bison, coyotes, and prairie dogs live in the Badlands. Visitors travel through the Badlands by car, on horseback, or on foot.

Little Town on the Prairie

Little Town on the Prairie is in De Smet. Laura Ingalls Wilder wrote five children's books about her childhood in De Smet. Visitors tour the author's childhood home. They see five cottonwood trees her father planted for Laura, her three sisters, and their mother.

Mount Rushmore National Memorial

Mount Rushmore National Memorial is in the Black Hills. The faces of four U.S. Presidents are carved into a mountain there. Nearly 400 people worked for 14 years to carve Mount Rushmore. Visitors follow the Presidential Trail to the base of the mountain.

Words to Know

agate (AG-it)—a hard stone with bands of color
carnivore (KAR-nuh-vor)—an animal that eats meat
dye (DYE)—a substance used to change the color of something such as a fabric
emblem (EM-bluhm)—a symbol or sign
fossil (FOSS-uhl)—plant or animal remains preserved in rock
furnace (FUR-niss)—a large machine that burns fuel to make heat
habitat (HAB-uh-tat)—the place and natural conditions where an animal usually lives
manufacturing (man-yuh-FAK-chur-ing)—the process of making something

Read More

Kummer, Patricia K. *South Dakota.* One Nation. Mankato, Minn.: Capstone Books, 1999.
McDaniel, Melissa. *South Dakota.* Celebrate the States. New York: Benchmark Books, 1998.
Thompson, Kathleen. *South Dakota.* Portrait of America. Austin, Texas: Raintree Steck-Vaughn, 1996.
Welsbacher, Anne. *South Dakota.* United States. Minneapolis: Abdo & Daughters, 1998.

Useful Addresses

Mount Rushmore
  National Memorial
P.O. Box 268
Keystone, SD 57751

South Dakota State
  Historical Society
900 Governors Drive
Pierre, SD 57501-2217

Internet Sites

Department of Tourism
http://www.travelsd.com
Mount Rushmore National Memorial
http://www.nps.gov/moru
Signs and Symbols of South Dakota
http://www.state.sd.us/state/sdsym.htm
South Dakota Historical Society
http://www.state.sd.us/state/executive/deca/cultural/
  sdshs.htm

Index